ICONS

To Penelope
My partner in life and travel.

To stay informed about upcoming TASCHEN titles, please request our magazine at www.taschen.com/magazine or write to TASCHEN America, 6671 Sunset Boulevard, Suite 1508, USA-Los Angeles, CA 90028, contact-us@taschen.com, Fax: +1-323-463.4442. We will be happy to send you a free copy of our magazine which is filled with information about all of our books.

Front cover, top:
Gizeh (Egypt), Pyramids of Cheops, 2250 BC
Front cover, bottom:
Niterói (Brazil), Contemporary Art Museum, 1996
Back cover, top:
New York (USA), Solomon R. Guggenheim Museum, 1959
Back Cover, bottom:
Angkor Thom (Cambodia), Bayon, ca. 1200

© 2004 TASCHEN GmbH
Hohenzollernring 53, D-50672 Köln
www.taschen.com

© text and photographs: Harry Seidler
Cover design: Sense/Net,
Andy Disl & Birgit Reber, Cologne

Printed in Italy
ISBN–13: 978–3-8228-3874-7
ISBN–10: 3-8228-3874-8

Harry Seidler's architectural sights

The Grand Tour

TASCHEN

HONGKONG KÖLN LONDON LOS ANGELES MADRID PARIS TOKYO

1 Karnak, Temple of Amun, 1550 BC

Hypostyle Hall with closely spaced huge columns, incised with figures and hieroglyphics.

2 Gizeh, Pyramids of Cheops, 2250 BC

Builder: Cheops

The very icons of ancient Egypt, these giant minimal sculptures stand in a sandy desert area near Cairo. The largest is 146.6 m high on a square base of 230 m, built of solid limestone blocks weighing some 2 tons each. The pyramid contains the King's, and below it, the Queen's burial chambers near its centre, reached by an internal sloping grand gallery, made of granite. Originally, the pyramids were covered in finely finished limestone with the peak reputed to have been covered in gold. All of this, however, was pillaged over the centuries.

3 Sakkara, 3000 BC

Entrance into a palace court with beautifully proportioned opening and recesses in the masonry surface.

4 Thebes, Temple of Queen Hatshepsut, 1550 BC

Architect: Senenmut

The setting of this terraced mortuary temple is spectacular. Rising from the Nile Valley it is approached by ramps to 3 levels toward the base of dramatic high rock cliffs. Double colonnades surround walled courts with fine incised relief sculptures.

2

1 Athens, Propylaea, 437-432 BC
Builder: Mnesikles
The entrance portico to the Acropolis.

2 Athens, Erectheion, 421-406 BC
Supporting Caryatid statue of a young
maiden, Erectheum, Athens.

3 Athens, Acropolis
Built on a platformed mountain.

2

3

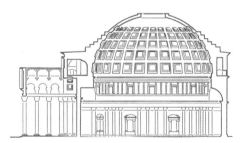

4

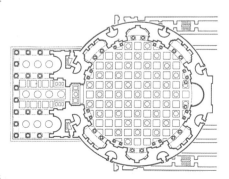

5

1 Rome, Colosseum, 70-82 AD

The most magnificent of many Roman amphitheatres, accommodated 60,000 spectators in an amazing engineering feat for its time.

2 Taormina Theatre

The originally Greek and later Roman Theatre overlooks the beautiful coast of Sicily.

3-5 Rome, The Pantheon, 118-126 AD

The circular building has the same diameter and height of about 50 m – an engineering triumph built in successively diminishing rings of stone with an open oculus in the centre.

6 Paestum, Temple of Neptune, 500 BC

The early best preserved Greek Temples. The Doric columns in the centre are heavier than later ones and are in superimposed two tiers.

7

8

9

10

11

7 Pisa, Dom St. Maria Assunta and The Leaning Tower, 12th Century

8 Venice, St Mark's, 13th Century
Campanile rebuilt after collapse in 1902.

9 Siena, Palazzo Publico Tower, 1300
Overlooking the public plaza. Famous for its yearly horse race, the Palio.

10 Bologna, Brick Towers, 1100
Torre Asinelli and Garisenda.

11 Senegalia
The fortifications on the Adriatic Coast.

12

13

14

15

16

17

18

19

12 Rome, Piazza del Popolo, 1670
Architect: C. Rainaldi
The central obelisk marks the converging point of three streets, flanked by two domed churches.

13 Rome, Piazza Navona, 1600's
Francesco Borromini's concave façade of the Sant' Agnese Church.

14 Florence, Ponte Veccio, 1345

20

15 Florence, Pitti Palace, 1460

16 Siena, 12th Century
Medieval tight network of narrow streets.

17 Siena Piazza del Campo, 14th Cent.
The open Campo, focus of the city.

18 Stra, Palace Pisani, 18th Century
The theatrical façade is merely a stable.

21

19 Venice, St Marks Square
The grandest urban space in Europe.

20 Rome, Piazza del Campidoglio, 1538
Architect: Michelangelo
The three buildings defining the trapezoidal plaza are placed apart to defy perspective and appear parallel.

21 Florence, Pazzi Chapel, 1429-61
Architect: Filippo Brunelleschi

22

22 Lucca
The oval-shaped central space follows the form of an ancient Roman amphitheatre.

23 Vigevano, 1492
Attributed to Donato Bramante. The painted facades reputed to be by Leonardo da Vinci.

24 Orvieto, Cathedral, 1290-1500
Architect: Arnolfo di Cambio
Has a quasi-Gothic façade decorated with colourful mosaics.

25 Rome, Tempietto, 1502
Architect: Donato Bramante
A High Renaissance small circular domed temple is built in the cloister of S. Pietro in Montorio.

26 Florence, S. Maria Novella, 1300
Architect: Leon Battista Alberti
The Renaissance façade of 1460.

27 Mantua, S. Andrea, 1470-76
Architect Leon Battista Alberti
The deeply recessed arched entry is one of the earliest Renaissance structures.

28 Venice, S. Zaccaria, 1450
Has a deeply moulded façade with beautiful arched roof forms.

29 Venice, Scuola di San Marco, 1490
Highlights of the arched elements of the façade are on either side of the entrance portals. Pictorial compositions in coloured marbles create perspective scenes, which appear to have a third dimension in depth.

24

25

26

27

28

29

31

30 Venice, Santa Maria della Salute, 1630
Architect: Baldassare Longhena

31 Turin, San Lorenzo, 1668-87
Architect: Guarino Guarini
Based on octagonal geometrics the plan
ends in a top-lit dome supported by eight
interlocking ribs.

32

33

34

5

2 Maser, Villa Barbaro, 1550
Architect: Andrea Palladio
A combined country house with farm
buildings.

3 Maser, Villa Barbaro, 1550
Architect: Andrea Palladio
Interior. The central wing has life-size
wall frescos by Paolo Veronese.

4 Vicenza, Basilica, 1549
Architect: Andrea Palladio
The façade with the typical "Palladian"
motive of Serliana openings of arches
and columns.

5 Fanzolo, Villa Emo, 1565
Architect: Andrea Palladio
As with Villa Barbaro, a combined
residence with arcaded access wings.

36

36 Rome, Palazetto dello Sport, 1957
Architect: Pier Luigi Nervi
This smaller of the two Olympic Stadia
built for the 1960 Games was constructed
of precast "ferro cement" pans, a system
invented by Nervi, to form interlocking
concrete ribs poured between them
to span large distances.
The building represents a rare fusion of
rational structure with a sculpturally
satisfying aesthetic result.

37 Mantua, Burgo Paper Mill, 1961
Architect: Pier Luigi Nervi
The 165 m span suspension structure
is carried by concrete trestles.

38 Turin, Palace of Labour, 1960
Architect: Pier Luigi Nervi
The cantilevered steel roof beams are
supported by expressively tapered
concrete columns.

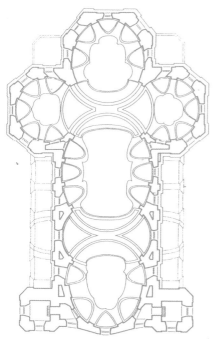

1-3 Vierzehnheiligen (Fourteen Saints), 1750

Architect: Balthasar Neumann
with the Monastery of Banz in the distance (by Johann L. Dienztenhofer). The pilgrimage church is a supreme example of Rococo architecture in Germany. While the exterior is relatively quiet, the interior bursts forth into a brilliant assembly of frescoed oval and elliptical vaults.

4

5

6

7

9

10

12

13

14

4 Neresheim, Monastery, 1745-64
Architect: Balthasar Neumann

5, 8 Munich, S. Johann Nepomuk, (Asamkirche), 1733-46
Architects: Asam Brothers

6, 7, 10, 11 Würzburg, Residenz Palace, 1750
Architect: Balthasar Neumann (and others)
The Chapel and Emperor's halls with frescoes by the celebrated Venetian painter Giovanni Battista Tiepolo.
The grand staircase of 1735 with the ceiling fresco also by Tiepolo are the most satisfying and grandiose works of German Baroque.

9 Weltenburg Abbey, 1716-39
Architects: Asam Brothers
This Benedictine abbey is distinguished by indirect natural light from above, with the effect of intense artificial spotlighting falling on the focal altar and central sculpture of St. George and the dragon. The impact is that of a dramatic stage setting.

12 Alfeld, Faguswerke, 1911-25
Architect: Walter Gropius

13 Stuttgart, Weissenhof Siedlung 1927
Architect: Le Corbusier

14 Berlin, New National Gallery, 1962-6
Architect: Mies van der Rohe

15 Dessau, Bauhaus, 1925-26
Architect: Walter Gropius
Not only did this building house an institute developing a new approach to architecture, industrial design and art, but it is a famous example of architecture expressive in its parts of diverse purposes. The workshop wing is fully glazed for maximum daylight. Classroom wings have continuous horizontal ribbon windows; the "Prellerhaus" students' studio and living quarters have individual balconies, etc.

1 Vendome Cathedral, 1300
This small flamboyant Gothic structure has flame-shaped window tracery and wide span flying buttresses.

2 Nimes, Pont du Gard, 19 BC
A spectacular Roman aqueduct engineering feat 50 m high. The supporting arch structure remains unadorned to serve purely its utilitarian purpose.

3 Toulouse, Les Jacobins, 1260
The early Gothic rib-vaulted roof is supported by a central row of columns, which culminate in a beautiful palm-tree like semi-circular apse end.

4

4 Paris, Notre-Dame Cathedral, started 1163
The high nave is braced by double span flying buttresses. Large circular transept stained glass windows are held by thin stone tracery.

5 Vézelay, S. Madeleine, 1089-1206
Romanesque Church with a high unadorned two-tone semi-circular stone arched nave.

6 Chartres Cathedral, 1220
The building with two unequal height towers is made famous by the magnificent predominantly blue stained glass windows.

7 Paris, Sainte-Chapelle, 1240
Architect: Pierre de Montrevil
A small court chapel, but very high for its width, almost entirely of 15 m high stained glass. The vaulted ceiling is decorated bright blue.

8 Beauvais Cathedral 1220 started, completed in the 16th Century
At 50 m it is the highest and widest of Gothic Cathedrals, plagued by structural failures and rebuilding during the long construction period. Only the apse end remains, which is awe inspiring with high clerestory windows.

6

8

9

9 Chambord, Chateau, start of construction 1590

Architect: Domenico da Cortona
Of all the 16th Century chateaus, this must be the most unbelievably bizarre, bristling with gables, pinnacles, domes and decorated chimneys surrounding a long turreted structure. Its ingenious central double spiral staircase allows a person walking up not to be seen by someone descending.

10 Chenonceau, Chateau, 1540

Built across the river, this elegant building with long galleries overlooking the tranquil water has a long history of jealousies of different Kings, their wives and mistresses.

11 Azay-le-Rideau Chateau, 1520

One of the most exquisite chateaus in the Valley of the Indre River. The nearest thing to a fairy tale castle is surrounded by water and superb forests.

10

11

13

4

5

12 Menier Chocolate Works, Noisiel-sur-Marne, 1879
Architect: Jules Saulnier
The first iron skeleton supported building with non-structural brick infill exterior walls.

13, 14 Paris, Métropolitain Stations, 1900
Architect: Hector Guimard
Art Nouveau cast iron and glass structures in organic decorative forms.

15 Paris, National Library, 1860
Architect: Henri Labrouste
The spherical roof vaults, each with a skylight, are supported by slim cast iron columns.

16

17

18

20

19

16, 18 Poissy, Villa Savoie, 1928-31
Architect: Le Corbusier
The iconic best known of the architect's houses, is built on a large property outside of Paris. The dramatic spatial fusion of the upper level hollow centre with access ramps and spiral stairs make this a supreme example of the fusion of art and architecture.

17 Villa Garches, 1926-28
Architect: Le Corbusier
This luxurious house built for the famous Stein family in the country near Paris represents an important milestone in Le Corbusier's work. It demonstrates the clear separation of structure and infill, enabling spaces to be free and open aesthetically, both horizontally and vertically. This seminal building has influenced architecture to this day.

19, 20 Paris, Villa La Roche-Jeanneret, 1923
Architect: Le Corbusier
An early duplex residence with interiors of spatial complexity. The building now houses the Le Corbusier Foundation.

21

83

85

21-23 The Chapel at Ronchamp, 1951-55
Architect: Le Corbusier

This represents a unique sculptural departure from conventional modern architecture. The awe-inspiring curvilinear interior receives daylight from various apertures in side-walls and top light through attached tower structures. The huge pivoted entrance is covered with a colourful metal mural by the architect.

24

24-26 Convent of La Tourette, 1953-60

Architect: Le Corbusier
The open central courtyard is surrounded
by monks' rooms and communal facilities.
A top lit colourful chapel is adjacent to the
large church hall.

27 Cheverny, Chateau, 1634

Architect: Comte Henri Hurault
Axially approached, the symmetrical
building's flat façade achieves distinction
from its varying height and shape roof
forms. One of the most elegant chateaus
in France.

28 Paris, Place des Vosges, 1605-12

Architect: Louis Metezeau
A fine urban square surrounded by arcaded
individual residential buildings, each with
its own roof. The two larger axial pavilions
are reserved for the King and Queen.

25

26

27

28

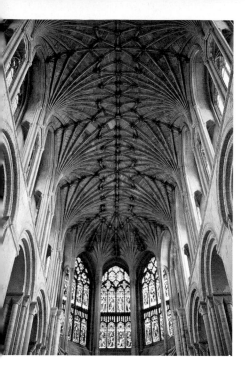

Bath, Prior Park, 1755
Architect: John Wood Snr
This fine property and bridge were
developed by the architect. The landscape
architecture was done by Capability Brown.

Norwich, Cathedral, 11th-14th Century
One of the finest of early English Gothic.

3

3 Ely, Cathedral Octagon, 14th Century
The central tower collapsed and was
replaced by the timber framed lantern.

4 Salisbury, Cathedral, 1220-56
Considered the purest of English Gothic
architecture it is cohesive in style, as it was
built in a short time.

5 London, Westminster Abbey, 1245

**6 London, Greenwich, The Royal Naval
College** by Christopher Wren with the
Queens House beyond by Inigo Jones,
1620.

4

7

7 London, Royal Opera Arcade, 1818
Architect: John Nash
Strong co-ordinated architectural forms
and cohesive timber shop fronts are
beautifully maintained.

8 London Zoo, Penguin Pool, 1934
Architect: Berthold Lubetkin and Tecton
An imaginative early use of thin reinforced
concrete curved slabs creates a sculptural
totality.

9 Bexhill, De La Warr Pavilion, 1935
Architects: Mendelsohn and Chermayeff
The community building is a rare
early example of distinguished modern
architecture in England.

10 Ironbridge, 1779
Engineer: Abraham Darby
The world's first iron bridge, which
revolutionised building methods.

11 London, British Museum, 2000
Architect: Norman Foster
The courtyard's flat glazed dome
inventively uses glass as a structural
compressive element.

12, 13 Bath, The Royal Crescent, 1767
Architect: John Wood the younger
This grandiose town planning assembly
of geometric building forms gives an
unprecedented cohesive character to the
whole town. The housing was built by the
Woods, as commercial development.

8

9

0

1

58

12

13

1

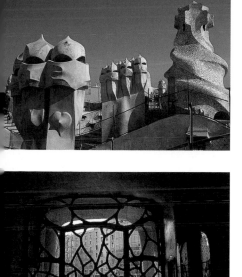

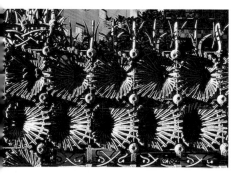

1 Barcelona, Casa Milà, 1906-10
Architect: Antoni Gaudí
Detail of Façade

2 Barcelona, Casa Milà, 1906-10
Architect: Antoni Gaudí
The rooftops sculptural chimneys.

3, 4 Barcelona, Casa Milà, 1906-10
Architect: Antoni Gaudí
The main entrance doors handmade of
beaten wrought iron.

5 Barcelona, Güell Pavilion, 1885
Architect: Antoni Gaudí
Iron fence.

**6, 8 Barcelona, La Sagrada Família, 1883
- still in construction**
Architect: Antoni Gaudí
This building is the landmark of Barcelona.
Long after Gaudí's death the interior
structure is finally being completed
following the original design but executed
in part using pre-cast concrete instead of
stone.

7 Barcelona, Casa Batlló, 1904
Architect: Antoni Gaudí
The curvilinear stone façade recalls
organic forms.

6

7

9

9, 11 Córdoba
For centuries the centre of Muslim Spain.
The huge arched mosque structure,
875-987 AD, had a Christian Cathedral
inserted in its centre in the 16th Century.

10 Córdoba
The 13th Century interlocking cross vaults
are reminiscent of Guarino Guarini's work
in 18th Century Turin.

10

12

13

4

2-14 Granada, The Alhambra, 1350

n elaborate and richly decorated Muslim
ortress palace with formal pavilions; the
on court and the arcaded Myrtles court
ith a central reflecting pool.

15-18 Barcelona, German Pavilion, 1929

Architect: Ludwig Mies van der Rohe

This ultimate icon of modern architecture was erected for the International exhibition in 1929, demolished after a mere three months and faithfully reconstructed permanently as a museum in 1986. The concentration of support in regularly placed steel columns allowed the free disposition, independently, of screen-like walls that create a continuum of flowing space between them. This spatial openness is dramatised by the use of the most sumptuous materials, polished marble, onyx, travertine and polished chrome. Two reflecting pools complete this dramatic demonstration of the new language in architecture, amplified by the architect's specially designed chairs, which have become famous internationally. There are no exhibits in the building, which in itself serves that purpose.

15

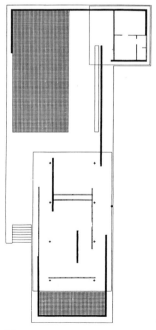

16

19 Bilbao, Guggenheim Museum, 1991-97

Architect: Frank Gehry

This amazing unprecedented sculptural building is made possible in our computer era which not only enables architects to draw such designs accurately, but by the computer instructing machines to produce all elements for assembly. There are virtually no straight or perpendicular lines in the building. The exterior is sheathed with panels of Titanium.

20, 21 Bilbao, Underground Station, 1991

Architect: Norman Foster

Approached through glass arched entries from street level, the upper station concourse is suspended from the wide precast concrete vaulted station roof.

22 Bilbao, Footbridge, 1997

Engineer: Santiago Calatrava

This extraordinary structure has the translucent glass walkway (dramatically lit from within at night) suspended from a one-sided tilting arch support.

1 Braga, Bom Jesus do Monte
Architect: Carlos Amarante
The twin towered 18th Century pilgrimage
church stands atop a granite and plaster
Baroque staircase, adorned with fountains
and terracotta statues. The form of this
long double stair built into the natural
hillside is one of the richest examples of
Baroque art.

2 Tomar, Azulejos Wall

3 Batalha, Cloister, 1500

**4 Belém, Monastery of Jeronimos,
1495-1521**
Architect: Diogo de Boytac
An example of Manueline Architecture
with distinctive rib vaulting and cloisters.

, 2 Utrecht, Schröder House, 1924
Architect: Gerrit Rietveld
The most famous of "De Stijl" buildings with
  flexible subdividable open interior is a
publicly accessible museum.
Opposing vertical and horizontal slab-like
walls and continuous glass areas create
compositions with their "tensional" window
sub-divisions which recall the work of
Dutch artists at the time.

3

4

3 Amsterdam, Open Air School, 1930
Architect: Johannes Duiker
An early reinforced concrete glazed
structure with cantilevered corners. The
building is as new, still used for its original
purpose.

4 Amsterdam, Stock Exchange, 1903
Architect: Hendrik Petrus Berlage
An early minimalist structurally expressive
brick building.

Rotterdam, van Nelle Factory, 1924
Architects: Brinkman & van der Vlugt
One of the earliest total glass curtain wall
buildings in Europe expressly designed for
the comfort and safety of employees.

1 Brussels, Solvay House, 1896
Architect: Victor Horta
The polished stone stair and walls are
combined with characteristic flat iron
ornate railing. They are in contrast to the
exposed riveted steel columns and beams.

2 Antwerp
The town square with touching gabled
facades.

3

4

5

3-5 Brussels, Horta House, 1898
Architect: Victor Horta
The central curved stair with flat iron decoration, gives access to split-level floors, creating a continuity of spatial effects. Walls are of bare glazed brick and tiles reaching the top floor with a curved glass skylight.

Helsinki, Central Railway Terminal, 1910
Architect: Eliel Saarinen
The solid granite building with Art Nouveau sculptures and decoration.

Helsinki, Lutheran Cathedral, 1830-52
Architect: Carl Engel
The glistening white classic building stands on a commanding hilltop.

3

4

3, 4 Paimio, Sanatorium, 1929-33
Architect: Alvar Aalto
Standing in a remote forest of tall pine trees, this present day fully functioning pristine white building complex, belies its age inside and out. The interiors are cheerfully bright and colourful.

5 Helsinki University of Technology, Otaniemi, 1966
Architect: Alvar Aalto
This large quadrant shaped building contains three lecture halls with steeply rising seating.

6 Helsinki, Finlandia Hall, open 1971
Architect: Alvar Aalto
Beautifully sited along a water frontage, the long building is surrounded by a park. The white marble clad exterior is in contrast to the warm tones of the interior. Round dark blue wall tiles are used to protect heavily trafficked areas.

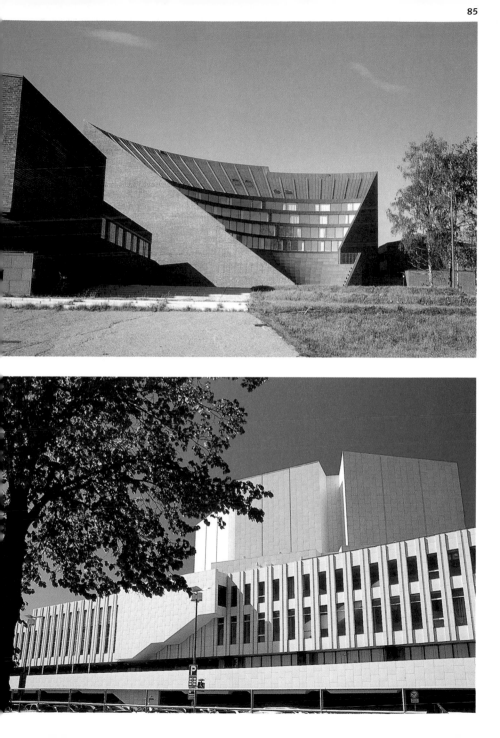

Vienna, Jesuit Church, 1626-31
The richly gilded interior is crowned
by a Trompe-L'-Oeil dome fresco by
Andrea Pozzo.

Krems
The town portal with Medieval and
Baroque decorative towers.

3

3 Vienna, Karlskirche, 1715
Architect: Fischer von Erlach
This amazing Baroque Church has a
classic temple portico flanked by two
freestanding minaret-like pylons leading
to a high oval domed interior.

4 Vienna, Piaristen Church, 1700
Architect: Lucas von Hildebrandt
The brilliant Baroque spatial interior has
indirect natural light reaching the central
nave from hidden overhead sources.

5

6

5 Vienna, Belvedere Palace, 1721
Architect: Lucas von Hildebrandt
Built for Prince Eugene of Savoy in gratitude after his defeat of the Turks who surrounded the city in 1683. The palace has a commanding view of Vienna over its formal gardens and fountains, which has not changed since Bellotto (called Canaletto) painted the scene in the 18th Century.

6 Vienna, Spanish Riding School,
18th Century
Architect: Fischer von Erlach
The white colonnaded wide span long hall is home to the unique performances of Lippizaner horses trained to do difficult jumps, steps and dances, all in unison with musical accompaniment.

7 Vienna, Karlsplatz Underground Station, 1898
Architect: Otto Wagner
The gilded iron framed structure holds walls of white marble panels, said to be the first non-weight bearing "curtain wall".

8 Vienna, Schönbrunn Palm House, 188-82
Architect: Franz von Segenschmid

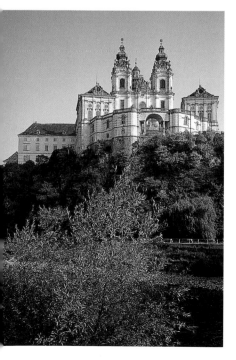

9 Melk, Benedictine Monastery, early 18th Century
Architect: Jacob Prandtauer
Dramatically sited on a high rocky ledge above the Danube, the monumental church interior is sumptuously gilded, as is the adjacent library.

10

10 Vienna, Postsparkasse, 1906
Architect: Otto Wagner
This most inventive and progressive building for its time has a glass roofed banking hall and specially designed air heating columns, light fixtures and furniture.
The thick granite exterior facing is secured with exposed metal bolts.

11 Vienna, Sezession Exposition Pavilion, 1898
Architect: Joseph Maria Olbrich
With the famous inscription "To each era its art and to art its freedom".

12 Vienna, Karl-Marx-Hof, 1926

Architect: Karl Ehn

One of the first of many public housing projects built by the City following the establishment of the Republic after World War I. 60% of the Viennese now live in such housing.

13 Vienna, Loos Haus, 1910

Architect: Adolf Loos

The first, totally undecorated façade opposite the Hofburg, the Imperial Palace offended the Emperor. The architect had to add window flower boxes.

3 Einsiedeln, Benedictine Abbey,
04-47

hitect: Kaspar Moosbrugger
minating the large town square, the
urch's unusual plan places the pilgrimage
a in the centre of a large oval entrance
ce. This results in a dramatically
iating arched support structure. To
rease the apparent depth of the nave
n iron screen, with lines imitating
spective effects.

4

4 Geneva, Vessy Bridge, 1936
Engineer: Robert Maillart
A seminal example by a pioneer of a
concrete structure that is expressive of
rational static forces and simultaneously
achieves fine visual results.

5 Moscia, Koerfer House, 1963
Architect: Marcel Breuer
Built on a rugged hillside commanding a
sweeping view of Lago Maggiore, the
concrete structure is exposed both inside
and out. It stands on granite rubble walls,
which fit the house into the terrain.

6 Zürich, La Maison de l'Homme, 1967
Architect: Le Corbusier
The exhibition pavilion is the result of th
private initiative of Heidi Weber and wa
built in a public park close to Zürich Lak
One of the few steel structures by Le
Corbusier, its form is defined by two
opposing umbrella-like roof forms. The
brightly coloured exterior panels contras
with the off-form concrete access ramp.

Prague, Charles Bridge, 1357-1402
Architect: Peter Parler
Connects the Old Town to the "Lesser" side
of Town. The bridge is lined with sculptures
on both sides, some of Saints, which were
a later addition.

Prague, St Nicholas Church, 1732-35
Architect: Christoph Ignac Dientzenhofer
A superbly flamboyant example of Baroque
architecture inside and out.

3

4 Zdar, St Nepomuk Church, 1722
Architect: Jan Santini

This five-sided domed church (a UNESCO Cultural Heritage) is based on extraordinary geometry, which changes from the inside to the richly sculptural exterior. Surrounding the churchyard is a typical Santini work with chapels of alternating concave and convex plan outlines.

5 Prague, St Vitus Cathedral, 14th Century
Architects: Peter Parler and Matthias of Arras

The structure spanning the high nave and crossing consists of exceptionally narrow columns and high clerestory, rising to interlocking ribbed vaults.

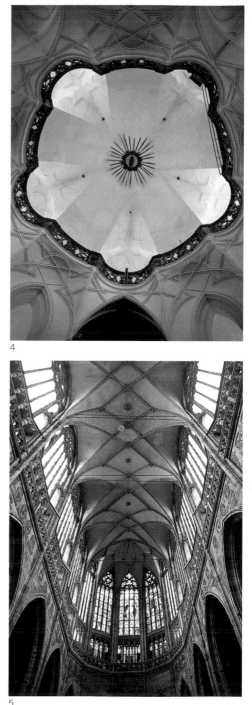

4

5

6-9 Brno, Tugendhat House, 1929

Architect: Ludwig Mies van der Rohe

This house built for the Tugendhat family in 1929 is one of Mies van der Rohe's masterpieces. The free-flowing spaces are made possible by the use of technologically advanced construction for its time, such as exposed chromed steel supports and enormous areas of glass, which can be electrically lowered down below the floor. Neglected and vandalised during World War II, it is now a faithfully restored house museum, furnished with the famous tables and chairs Mies designed specially for the house. Onyx and Palisander screen walls create a sumptuously elegant atmosphere, which is an icon in modern architecture.

6

7

Budapest, Museum of Applied Arts, 83-1896
chitect: Ödön Lechner
rvilinear central interior space, to
phasise the eastern origin of the country.

Budapest, 19th Century
etal gate entry into the Royal Buda Palace.

Budapest, Neo Gothic Parliament ilding "Orszaghaz", 1885-1902
chitect: Imre Steindl
ilt on a dramatic waterfront site facing
e Danube.

Mostar, Bosnia-Herzegovina
he town along both sides of the river
ocuses on the 14th century footbridge,
hich was destroyed in 1993, but restored
2001-04.

Pristina, Kosovo
fine interlocking vaulted arch stone
hurch.

**Moscow, Kremlin, Assumption
Cathedral, 1470**
The beautifully proportioned arched façade
is crowned with gold surfaced circular
towers.

**St. Petersburg, Hermitage Winter
Palace, 1754-62**
Architect: Bartolomeo Francesco Rastrelli
The long building facing the river on one
side and the historic square on the other,
is a sumptuously appointed structure with
internal courtyards.

3

4

3, 4 St. Petersburg, Hermitage
The monumental entrance with gilded decor.

5 St. Petersburg
The reconstructed Peterhof Palace with fountains playing and ballet dancers performing celebrating an anniversary.

6 Smolny, Cathedral and Convent, 1748-64
Architect: Bartolomeo Francesco Rastrelli
The Cathedral is the centrepiece of the large group of buildings. Rastrelli aimed to combine Baroque detail with a forest of onion domes of a traditional Russian monastery.

7

7 Moscow, Red Square
The focal point of the city, with the colourfully decorated domes of St. Basil's Cathedral and people lining up to see Lenin's tomb.

8 Moscow, GUM Department Store, 1895
Architect: Alexander Pomerantsev
Along Red Square, is an elaborate complex of iron and glass vaulted shopping galleries

9, 10 Moscow
Underground Stations, built in the 1930's with elaborate traditional marble decoration to evoke an atmosphere of palatial splendour for the masses of users.

Istanbul, Mosque of Sultan Ahmed (Blue Mosque), 1609-16
Architect: Mehmet Aga
The forecourt is surrounded by a domed arcade leading into a square structure with heavy supporting piers. Six minarets add to a finely proportioned totality.

Istanbul, Hagia Sophia, 6th Century

Istanbul, Hagia Sophia, 6th Century
This enormous church interior with its suspended central dome is a heroic structural feat for its time.

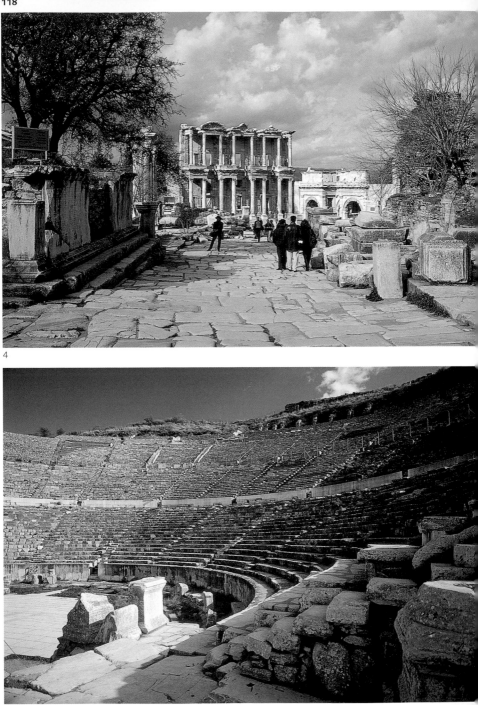

4

5

, 6 Ephesus, The Library of Celsus,
60 AD

he reconstruction and preservation of
he façade were conducted by Prof.
riedmund Hueber of the Austrian
rchaeological Institute. Alternating
urved and triangular pediments above
nd flat offset entablatures below are
arried by columns, which create a
cintillating façade composition.

Ephesus

he Roman amphitheatre built into
aturally sloping ground.

6

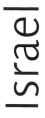

erusalem, The Western or "Wailing all", 20 BC

a remnant of the temple destroyed in
 AD. The grand public space in front of
e wall is the most revered urban area of
e city. The gilded "Dome of the Rock"
0 AD is seen in the left background.

**erusalem, The Israel Museum Shrine
the Books, depository of the Dead
a Scrolls, 1965**

*hitects: Friedrich Kiesler and Armand
rtos*

e accessible form of the Museum Hall
based on the profile of the ancient
ntainer in which the scrolls were found.
e arresting sculptural exterior is clad in
ss white ceramics.

erusalem

e Billy Rose sculpture garden in the Israel
useum. Freestanding screen walls form
open spatial environment through which
itors can stroll. The screen walls create
ackground for each individual work of
, without visual distraction.

2

3

1

Petra, Treasury, 1st Century AD
ɔproaching through the Siq, a 1.2 km
ng narrow gorge and suddenly coming
ɔon this rock-cut building is the ultimate
rill of discovery for the visitor.

Qasr-Kharana
anding alone in a treeless desert area this
ɪpressive building has finely proportioned
:posed stone walls. The internal spaces
ce an open central court.

Isfahan
...e Masjit-i-Imam with typical geometric
...peated ceramic surfaces, which permit
...finite numbers of permutations.

Isfahan, Imam Mosque, 1612-30
...flected at the end of the water filled
...eydan focal square of Isfahan.

Taroudant
The town is surrounded by magnificent
crenellated red mud walls.

Ait Benhaddou, Kasbah
An impressive assembly of tapered high
towers surrounding courtyards with high
walls.

World Trade Center Towers, 1966-73

Architect: Minoru Yamasaki

For some 30 years the 100-storey twin office towers were the most visible landmarks of Manhattan. On September 11, 2001, they were destroyed in a terrorist attack by jet aircraft being driven into their sides, causing an inferno, which killed some 3,000 people.

When visiting the buildings during construction in 1970, I remember being amazed at the exclusive use of lightweight building materials. Their steel structure consisted of closely spaced exterior columns and 20 m floor beams spanning to the elevator core. No concrete was used around firestairs or elevator shafts instead, layers of plasterboard were chosen. The immense heat generated by the impact explosion of jet fuel, weakened the steel structure to such an extent that it caused the progressive collapse of both towers in short time.

New York, Rockefeller Center, 1929-40

Architects: Reinhard & Hofmeister with Raymond Hood

Simultaneously with the Empire State and the Chrysler Tower, this landmark of New York was built during the Great Depression. It consists of nine various height buildings with the 70-storey RCA Tower its centre-piece. What is admirable in the complex are the large open pedestrian spaces which have remained a magnet attracting people its malls and plazas.

Charlottesville, Va., University of Virginia, 1819-26

Architect: Thomas Jefferson

The symmetrical U-shaped central space terminates in the Roman Pantheon-like library building in this serenely beautiful environment. Five double-storey pavilions connected by low classical colonnades contain teaching and living accommodation.

4

4 Oak Park, Ill., Unity Temple, 1905-07

Architect: Frank Lloyd Wright

One of the first "binuclear" or "H plans" later used extensively by others, whereby the main hall and subsidiary spaces are separate and connected with a narrowed entrance link. The powerful solid concrete building has a clear structural expression i the hall, emphasised by the source of daylight. Deep glazed coffers in the roof and horizontal windows placed between the corner supporting elements.

5, 7 Chicago, Ill., Robie House, 1908-09

Architect: Frank Lloyd Wright

This is one of Wright's most famous work characterised by hugely cantilevered low slung roof planes, interlocking volumes ar planes and sweeping horizontals.

6 Chicago, Ill., The Rookery, 1885-88

Architects: Daniel H. Burnham, John Wellborn Root, Frank Lloyd Wright (reconstruction)

The exposed iron structure supporting the central glazed court's roof is an example progressive engineering design in the 19t Century.

8 Los Angeles, Cal., Lovell House, 1927-29

Architect: Richard Neutra

This well-known house is one of the first examples of uncompromising modern architecture in America. Its light steel fram construction and multi-level spacious inte iors influenced much later design in the U.S. and Europe.

9 Palm Springs, Cal., Kaufmann House, 1946-47

Architect: Richard Neutra

Based on a pin-wheel plan, the different wings allow individual panoramic views o the surrounding mountains and desert scenery to every room.

5

10 Bear Run, Pa., Fallingwater, Kaufmann House, 1935-39

Architect: Frank Lloyd Wright

This is Wright's world-famous house, cantilevered over a gushing waterfall in the most beautiful wild natural setting. The vertical rough stone piers support daringly hovering horizontal concrete elements of terraces and suspended spaces. Even though romantic in character, the off-white house is clearly influenced by European modern architecture of the time.

11

12

11-13 New York, Solomon R. Guggenheim Museum, 1943-59

Architect: Frank Lloyd Wright

Wright's most celebrated building is based on an extraordinary concept, some 15 years in development. The central top lit atrium is surrounded by spiral gallery spaces, which were much criticised due to the sloping floors and limited ceiling height. With the completion of Wright's original rectilinear wing, with high spaces (Architect: C. Gwathmey) the museum functions well and is more popular than ever.

14 New York, Museum of Modern Art, 1939

Architects: Philip Goodwin & Edward Durrell Stone

This culturally important museum started as a plain translucent stone fronted structure. It has undergone many alterations and additions over the years, the best of which is the fine sculpture garden by Philip Johnson.

15

16

7

18

15 Washington D.C., Dulles International Airport, 1958-62

Architect: Eero Saarinen

The sweeping catenary roof structure is supported by outward leaning concrete pylons and steel tension cables hung between them, resulting in a huge column-free space.

16 Chicago, Ill., Crown Hall, I.I.T., 1950-56

Architect: Mies van der Rohe

The main floor of this architecture school consists of a single large space, supported by an external steel frame and enveloped in glass. It is one of Mies' most expressive concepts of a powerful minimal structure.

17 Washington D.C., East Wing, National Gallery of Art, 1968-78

Architect: Ieoh Ming Pei

The basis of this superbly designed monumental building is triangular geometry and forms derived from it.

18 New York, Whitney Museum of American Art, 1966

Architect: Marcel Breuer

Placed on a small corner site, the grey granite clad square building steps out toward the top to leave space for an outdoor sculpture court below street level. Unique trapezoidal windows admit daylight to the gallery floors.

19

20

1

19, 20 Collegeville, Minn., St John's Abbey and University, 1953-61

Architect: Marcel Breuer

The folded concrete Abbey Church is supported by ground level columns with glass walls between that admit daylight to the monumental interior which is tapered both vertically and horizontally. The dramatic freestanding bell banner straddles the entrance.

21, 22 Fort Worth, Tex., Kimbell Museum of Art, 1966-72

Architect: Louis Kahn

Composed of six parallel concrete vaults which span the whole length of the structure, the "servant" spaces between them allowed variations of displays between the top lit galleries within the long vaults.

22

23

24

5

3, 24 New Canaan, Conn., Glass House, 949

rchitect: Philip Johnson
)n a visit in 1955, Marcel Breuer (see
holo) look me to see this steel framed
lass pavilion. It was the first of such totally
lazed houses in the USA. It is built in an
xtensive park-like setting and was later
oined by other small buildings, a sculpture
avilion, an underground museum and a
uest house.
lies van der Rohe had sketched such a
lass house in 1934 and built the elegant
arnsworth House in Plano, Ill. in 1951.

25 Lincoln, Mass., Walter Gropius House, 1938

Architects: Walter Gropius & Marcel Breuer
This revolutionary house is the first work
by these two recently appointed influential
Harvard Professors. The simple rectilinear
outline of the building is sculpted with
hollowed out, recessed spaces, stone
walls and screens. The angled entrance
is recalled in an opposing slanting wall in
the living area.
Other than in books, it is the first deeply
impressive masterpiece of modern
architecture that Gropius' students have
seen (including myself).
Photo 25, the 1946 photo is the earliest
taken, in this book.

1 Mexico City, Centro National de las Artes, 1994
Architect: Ricardo Legorreta
The access stair, leading to the buildings of the centre, is typical of Mexican modern architecture which uses brilliant coloured walls.

2 Mexico City, Satellite City Towers, 1957
Architect: Luis Barragán and Artist:
Mathias Goeritz
These five towers were designed as a landmark for a new satellite city. They stand on an open plaza in the centre of an expressway. Their varying heights, 30 to 50 metres, and different triangular shapes and bright colours create a powerful image.

3 Chichén Itzá, Pyrámide de Kukulkan, 800 AD
A fine geometric silhouette stone building is of Mayan religious significance with sacred vault spaces within.

4

5

4 Chichén Itzá, 1000 AD
Surrounding stone buildings are seen from the top of the Pyramid; the long parallel walls of a ball court with projecting stone "goal" rings and the "Temple of the Warriors" with a remaining group of a Thousand stone columns.

5 Mitla
14th Century Zapotec recessed stone carved opposing patterns.

6 Uxmal, C600-900 AD
The well preserved stone buildings are of most impressive architectural design. The site planning and disposition of the structures create admirable spaces and vistas between them.

7 Teotihuacan, 150 - 600 AD
The site for this ancient Aztec city is 50 km north of Mexico City. It was once the capital of Mexico's largest Pre-Hispanic empire. The focal structures in this vast linear development are two pyramids, the largest 70 metres high, is dedicated to the sun, the smaller to the moon. The surrounding stepped structures were once colourfully painted.

8

9

9, 10 Mexico City, San Cristobal Stable and House, 1968

Architect: Luis Barragán

This large complex of brilliantly coloured freestanding pavilions, house, stables and screen walls, create a rich spatial-sculptured totality. A pond and gushing fountain are in the exercise yard for the owners' thoroughbred horses.

Mexico City, Luis Barragán's Own House, 1947

10

This unassuming modest house of the architect is full of surprises in the complex interior spaces and their natural light sources. The library's minimal composition has an open timber stair reaching the upper floor between two opposing white walls.

11 Mexico City, Casa Gilardi Indoor Swimming Pool, 1978

Architect: Luis Barragán

The pool is composed of blue, red and white smooth and textured wall and column surfaces. The colours change with the ripple of the water and create an unexpected translucence. To the user it must be a swimming experience through a work of art.

11

12 Mexico City, San Angel Casa Prieto Lopez, 1950

Architect: Luis Barragán

This house has a typical Mexican entry courtyard surrounded by brightly coloured walls. The inside spaces interact beautifully with large single pane windows opening into tranquil gardens.

12

13 Mexico City, Olympic Sports Palast, 1968

Engineer: Felix Candela

The ingenious space frame structure expresses its triangulated protruding elements, which results in a uniquely sculptural exterior.

13

São Paulo, Copan Building, 1951
Architect: Oscar Niemeyer

This co-operative apartment building takes on a wave-shaped plan form to fit onto the irregular inner city site. Two continuous horizontal louvres to each floor act as effective sun protection and afford privacy to the inhabitants.

São Paulo, Memorial of the Latin American States, 1990
Architect: Oscar Niemeyer

The large urban site contains an assembly plaza with a symbolically bleeding open hand sculpture by Niemeyer. Crisp white freestanding buildings surround the space. Their long span concrete structures create an interactive sculptural totality.

Brasilia, The Capital, 1957-60
Architect: Oscar Niemeyer

This focal point of Brazil's new capital places the two national Congress chambers on a platform. Their opposing convex and concave circular forms with the dual administrative towers between them, result in the iconical silhouette of the city.

4

5

6

4-6 Niteroi, Contemporary Art Museum, 1996

Architect: Oscar Niemcyer

Built on a peninsular reaching into Rio's harbour, the form and structure of this incredible building borders on the unbelievable. Prestressed radial interior ribs emanate from its central supporting hollow ring column. The upward sweep of the mushroom shaped glazed exterior wall runs parallel to the 'Sugarloaf' mountain in the distance.

7 São Paulo, Memorial of the Latin American States, 1990

Architect: Oscar Niemeyer

3 Kyoto, Katsura Palace, 1663

Architect: Kobori Enshu

The masterpiece of serene simplicity is set in harmony with a picturesque landscape environment. The restrained minimalism of the timber building consists only of supporting columns and an open planned interior which can be subdivided, opened or closed to the outside with their sliding panels, to serve diverse uses.

The garden surroundings are contrived to idealise nature and brings water, stepping stones, paths and plants into a romantic scene of perfection.

The unornamented interiors are devoid of western furniture, with a bare geometric order created by the use of multiple tatami rice-straw floor mats.

**Kyoto, The Golden Pavilion, 1397,
built 1950's**
⁣e gilded shrine is built in a park
⁣rrounded by water. It exudes an
⁣mosphere of untouchable perfection.

Kyoto, Heian Shrine, 1882
⁣e large overhanging roof and widely
⁣aced columns mark the entrance to
⁣series of courtyards within.

**7 Tokyo, The Imperial Hotel, 1916-
⁣22 (demolished 1967)**
⁣chitect: Frank Lloyd Wright
⁣nelope and I stayed in the hotel just
⁣fore its demolition. All interiors and
⁣rniture, designed by Wright, were still
⁣tact. The entrance hall was the most
⁣markable space in the huge complex.
⁣ had seven different levels, interacting
⁣atially and all merging into the entrance
⁣yer. Built of brick and carved lava stone,
⁣e structure was supported on an
⁣genious system of driven piles, which

saved the building in the disastrous 1923
earthquake.

**8 Takamatsu, Kagawa Prefecture,
1955-58**
Architect: Kenzo Tange
Solidly built of exposed textured concrete,
the modern office building recalls traditional
Japanese ponds with sculptural stone
blocks.The projecting concrete floor beams
are reminiscent of early timber structures.

6

7

Beijing, Temple of Heaven
he colourful carved timber ceiling structure
f the circular Temple of Heaven shrine.

Hong Kong, Bank of China Tower, 982-90
rchitect: Ieoh Ming Pei
his landmark of the city has a triangulated
xposed steel frame which expresses the
ʰrce dimensional form of the structure.

Beijing, Great Wall of China.
uccessive emperors ordered The Great
Vall of China to be constructed, protecting
ʰe country from Northern incursions.
he wall was started between the seventh
ɔ the fifth centuries B.C. and was
ontinuously strengthened over the ages
ɔ become 7m high and wide, built on
n internal earth core, faced with brick
xteriors on a stone base. The huge wall,
ɔme 6000 km long, winds up and down
cross the mountainous landscape. Its
cale is unparalleled in the architecture
f fortifications.

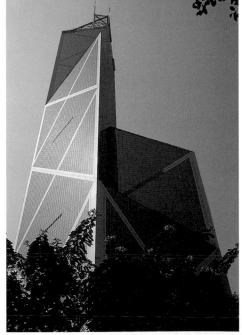

4

5

-9 Beijing, The Forbidden City, 1400

This imperial palace housed the emperors from the fourteenth until the early twentieth centuries and consists of a virtual city with halls, pavilions and towers covering a walled compound of some 720,000 square metres, which takes more than half an hour to traverse. Buildings face a series of large courtyards interrupted by temple structures, residence halls and religious shrines. On my second visit, in 1977, new snow fell at night and offered a unique view of the first snow covered large court, the only space containing a curvilinear watercourse and stone foot bridges.

6

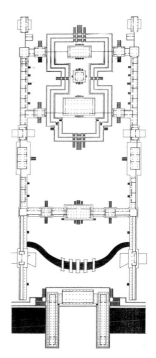

7

8

Java, Parambanan

Java, Borobudur

he most memorable of temples is the
erraced solid stone square pyramid, with
tatues, relief carvings and "stupas" rising
long continuously winding terraces and
teep steps to the 34 metre high roof.
he tallest inverted, 8 metre high stupa
orms the top and is ringed with smaller
erforated, inverted bell-like enclosures,
ach containing a sculptured Buddha with
different aspect and gesture.

1

Agra Fort, Khass Mahal, 1565
This white marble pavilion housed the
private apartments of the Emperor.

Agra Fort
Carved marble surrounds the pool and
scalloped arches support the pavilion.

Agra, Taj Mahal, 1631-1657
Architect: Isa Khan
The mausoleum was constructed by
Emperor Shah Jahan in memory of his
deceased wife.
This world famous white marble iconic
building has a graceful composition,
arrangement of a central dome, towers
and pointed arches, all raised on a
podium and focused on an axial reflecting
watercourse.

5

4 Udaipur, Lake Palace, by Maharana Jagat Singh II, 1754

Located in the centre of Udaipur and built on an island in the lake, this formal royal palace must be the most romantic, superbly crafted and extravagant creation anywhere. Surrounded by stone arched pavilions facing the water, its central courtyards are filled with lotus ponds and swimming pools. The palace is now used as a luxury hotel.

5 Agra, Itimad Ud Daulah (The Small Taj), 1622-1628

This is the first white marble temple built with inlaid precious stones, foreshadowing the Taj Mahal, a building using beautiful geometric proportions and perforated stone grille exteriors.

6

6-8 Fatehpur Sikri, 1571-85

Capital of the Mughal, Emperor Akbar.
This is among the finest cities built by
edict of an Indian Emperor in the 16th
century. The interlocking layout of various
size open spaces, watercourses, ringed
and punctuated by freestanding skilfully
positioned structures, all provide
constantly changing vistas as one strides
through this amazing city. Built of durable
red sandstone, some opposing white
marble pavilions, perforated screens and
fine workmanship, it is still something of a
mystery why it was deserted so soon
after its completion. The only explanation
offered is the problem of water supply
for its population. This cohesive complex
creates a beautiful totality without equal.

9

9 Jaipur, Jantar Mantar (or Observatory), 1728

10 Chandigarh, The Parliament building
Architect: Le Corbusier
The Parliament building is seen with the foothills of the Himalayas in the distance. The two chambers of government are in the centre of the building, projecting far above the roof and surrounded by circulation space.
Offices are planned against the exterior walls, covered with sun protection blades.

11 The Secretariat building is
254 meters long and 42 meters high, with the ramped pedestrian access tower projecting from the façade. The continuous repetitive sun protected office galleries are interrupted by irregular height ministerial offices and formal meeting spaces, all of which, including the office's proportions, are based on Le Corbusier's modular system.

0

1

12

12 Ahmedabad, Shodhan House, 1951
Architect: Le Corbusier
Following the construction of Chandigarh,
some industrialists in the city of
Ahmedabad invited Le Corbusier to build
houses and the headquarters of the
Millowners organisation. The most
dramatic of these is the Villa Shodhan,
a 3 storey building of sculptural plasticity
and penetrating spaces intertwining
exteriors and interiors, with modular
proportioned glass and solid infill walls.

13 Ahmedabad, Millowners' Association Building, 1954
Architect: Le Corbusier
Overlooking a river edge, the street
approach leads over an inclined ramp
into the open central space, to the offices
and meeting halls. Both east and west
facades are protected by brise-soleil from
the strong sunlight. The form-boarded
concrete gives a rugged texture to the
entire structure.

Angkor Thom, Bayon
ne of many enigmatically smiling carved
ads.

Banteay Srei, 10th Century
is Hindu temple is decorated with
autiful filigree carved reliefs depicting
ities.

3

3 Angkor Wat
Entrance causeway with tower structures.

4 Angkor Wat
Tower structure rising from courtyard and
ground plan showing central structures and
open courts.

5 Angkor Thom, Bayon, 1200
Entry from reflecting pool.

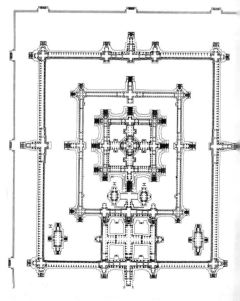

Sydney, Opera House, 1957-73
Architect: Joern Utzon

This design won an international
architectural competition. Its unique
precast concrete ribbed structure is
covered with glazed white tiles. After
structural completion, there was a dispute
between Utzon and the newly elected
state government client, following which
the architect was dismissed in 1966,
never to return.

Sydney, The Mint, 1814
Typical colonial era building with
colonnaded verandahs.

100 Houses for 100 Architects
Gennaro Postiglione (Ed.) / Flexi-
cover, 480 pp. / € 29.99 /
$ 39.99 / £ 19.99 / ¥ 5.900

Architecture Now! Vol. III
Philip Jodidio / Flexi-cover,
576 pp. / € 29.99 / $ 39.99 /
£ 19.99 / ¥ 5.900

Architecture Now! Vol. IV
Philip Jodidio / Flexi-cover,
576 pp. / € 29.99 / $ 39.99 /
£ 19.99 / ¥ 5.900

"TASCHEN books are beautiful, original, unpredictable, and affordable." —*The Observer Life Magazine*, London

"Buy them all and add some pleasure to your life."

African Style
Ed. Angelika Taschen

Alchemy & Mysticism
Alexander Roob

All-American Ads 40ˢ
Ed. Jim Heimann

All-American Ads 50ˢ
Ed. Jim Heimann

All-American Ads 60ˢ
Ed. Jim Heimann

American Indian
Dr. Sonja Schierle

Angels
Gilles Néret

Architecture Now!
Ed. Philip Jodidio

Art Now
Eds. Burkhard Riemschneider,
Uta Grosenick

Atget's Paris
Ed. Hans Christian Adam

Berlin Style
Ed. Angelika Taschen

Cars of the 50s
Ed. Jim Heimann, Tony
Thacker

Cars of the 60s
Ed. Jim Heimann, Tony
Thacker

Cars of the 70s
Ed. Jim Heimann, Tony
Thacker

Chairs
Charlotte & Peter Fiell

Christmas
Ed. Jim Heimann, Steven Heller

Classic Rock Covers
Ed. Michael Ochs

Design Handbook
Charlotte & Peter Fiell

Design of the 20ᵗʰ Century
Charlotte & Peter Fiell

Design for the 21ˢᵗ Century
Charlotte & Peter Fiell

Devils
Gilles Néret

Digital Beauties
Ed. Julius Wiedemann

Robert Doisneau
Ed. Jean-Claude Gautrand

East German Design
Ralf Ulrich / Photos: Ernst Hedler

Egypt Style
Ed. Angelika Taschen

Encyclopaedia Anatomica
Ed. Museo La Specola
Florence

M.C. Escher

Fashion
Ed. The Kyoto Costume
Institute

Fashion Now!
Ed. Terry Jones, Susie Rushton

Fruit
Ed. George Brookshaw,
Uta Pellgrü-Gagel

HR Giger
HR Giger

Grand Tour
Harry Seidler

Graphic Design
Eds. Charlotte & Peter Fiell

Greece Style
Ed. Angelika Taschen

Halloween
Ed. Jim Heimann, Steven
Heller

Havana Style
Ed. Angelika Taschen

Homo Art
Gilles Néret

Hot Rods
Ed. Coco Shinomiya, Tony
Thacker

Hula
Ed. Jim Heimann

Indian Style
Ed. Angelika Taschen

India Bazaar
Samantha Harrison, Bari Kumar

Industrial Design
Charlotte & Peter Fiell

Japanese Beauties
Ed. Alex Gross

Krazy Kids' Food
Eds. Steve Roden,
Dan Goodsell

Las Vegas
Ed. Jim Heimann,
W. R. Wilkerson III

London Style
Ed. Angelika Taschen

Mexicana
Ed. Jim Heimann

Mexico Style
Ed. Angelika Taschen

Morocco Style
Ed. Angelika Taschen

New York Style
Ed. Angelika Taschen

Paris Style
Ed. Angelika Taschen

Penguin
Frans Lanting

20ᵗʰ Century Photography
Museum Ludwig Cologne

Photo Icons I
Hans-Michael Koetzle

Photo Icons II
Hans-Michael Koetzle

Pierre et Gilles
Eric Troncy

Provence Style
Ed. Angelika Taschen

Robots & Spaceships
Ed. Teruhisa Kitahara

Safari Style
Ed. Angelika Taschen

Seaside Style
Ed. Angelika Taschen

Albertus Seba. Butterflies
Irmgard Müsch

**Albertus Seba. Shells &
Corals**
Irmgard Müsch

Signs
Ed. Julius Wiedemann

South African Style
Ed. Angelika Taschen

Starck
Philippe Starck

Surfing
Ed. Jim Heimann

Sweden Style
Ed. Angelika Taschen

Sydney Style
Ed. Angelika Taschen

Tattoos
Ed. Henk Schiffmacher

Tiffany
Jacob Baal-Teshuva

Tiki Style
Sven Kirsten

Tuscany Style
Ed. Angelika Taschen

Valentines
Ed. Jim Heimann,
Steven Heller

Web Design: Best Studios
Ed. Julius Wiedemann

Web Design: Flash Sites
Ed. Julius Wiedemann

Web Design: Portfolios
Ed. Julius Wiedemann

**Women Artists
in the 20ᵗʰ and 21ˢᵗ Century**
Ed. Uta Grosenick